flavouring with
Herbs

flavouring with
Herbs

Clare Gordon-Smith

photography by

James Merrell

RYLAND
PETERS
& SMALL

LONDON NEW YORK

Art Director **Jacqui Small**

Art Editor **Penny Stock**

Design Assistant **Lucy Hamilton**

Editor **Elsa Petersen-Schepelern**

Photography **James Merrell**

Food Stylist **Clare Gordon-Smith**

Stylist **Wei Tang**

Production Manager **Kate Mackillop**

Our thanks to Christine Walsh, Ian Bartlett and Poppy Gordon-Smith

First published in the Great Britain in 1996 by
Ryland Peters & Small
Kirkman House
12–14 Whitfield Street, London W1T 2RP
www.rylandpeters.com

This paperback edition first published in 2003
10 9 8 7 6 5 4 3 2 1

Text © Clare Gordon-Smith 1996
Design and photographs © Ryland Peters & Small 1996

Printed and bound in China

ISBN 1 84172 440 8

A CIP record for this book is available from the British Library

Notes:
Metric and imperial measurements are
given. Use one set of measurements
only and not a mixture of both.

Ovens should be preheated to the
specified temperature – if using a
fan-assisted oven, adjust time and
temperature according to the
manufacturer's instructions.

The flavours of herbs **6**

Starters **10**

Fish **22**

Meat and poultry **32**

Vegetarian **48**

Sweet things **60**

Index **64**

Herbs have been used through history for both cooking and medicinal purposes. Traditional herbs – parsley, sage, rosemary and thyme – have been joined by other favourites, such as tarragon, basil, mint, dill, bay leaves, oregano, chives and chervil, in an eclectic mix of flavouring ingredients. Modern-day cooks also use herbs from the cuisines of China, India and South-east Asia. Widely available in greengrocers' shops and supermarkets – sold either in bunches or growing in little pots – fresh herbs are now within everyone's reach.

Shown here (back row, from left) is a small bay tree, providing bay leaves, one of the most traditional herbs, an infusion of herbs in red wine vinegar, and lavender-flavoured sugar, which is used in baking.

Front row, from left, is a bundle of **Asian herbs**, now widely used in modern cooking, consisting of lemongrass, kaffir lime leaves, and coriander; a hot infusion of herbs in olive oil makes a quick dressing for a warm salad, and is also delicious sprinkled over boiled or roasted vegetables. Far right is one of the best of all herb flavourings – **pesto**, usually made with basil, garlic, pine nuts, and olive oil. Inspired chefs have made innovative changes, using rocket, parsley, or even coriander instead of basil, to give more unusual flavours.

the flavours of

Herbs

Marjoram Oregano Basil Thyme Chervil Lavender

Mint Lemon thyme Rosemary Bay leaves

Herbs are important flavouring ingredients in all the world's great cuisines. Rosemary, thyme and lavender grow wild on the hot, stony hillsides of the South of France, and have been enthusiastically adopted by cooks working in the western tradition. Chives, chervil and marjoram are widely used in European cuisines. Oregano is marjoram's wild cousin, and is typically used in Greek cooking. Dill, with its feathery leaves, its close relation fennel, and curly parsley are all traditional herbs used in Northern European cooking. Flat leaf parsley, more commonly used in Italy, is thought to have better flavour than its

8 The flavours of herbs

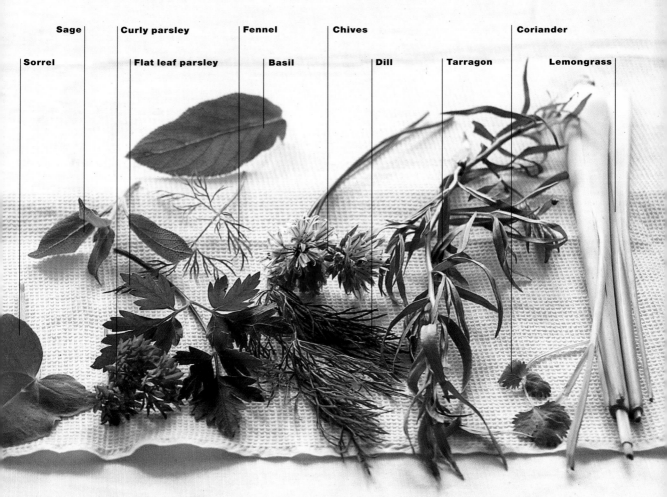

Sage	Curly parsley	Fennel	Chives	Coriander
Sorrel	Flat leaf parsley	Basil	Dill	Tarragon	Lemongrass

crinkly cousin. Other Italian favourites are sweet basil and tarragon. Of the hundreds of different varieties of mint, the most widely used are spearmint and the peppery-tasting Asian mint. They are part of traditional cuisines ranging from Europe to the Middle East, India and South-east Asia – and in the mint juleps of Kentucky. Lemongrass and coriander are widely used in the delicious cuisines of Thailand and Vietnam. Though dried herbs are traditional in some dishes, such as lasagne, fresh herbs have been used throughout this book for their finer flavour. If using dried herbs, halve the quantities given.

Starters

Sweet potato soup
with chive mascarpone cream

Sweet potatoes produce a soup with wonderful colour, sweet flavour and dense texture. This one is topped with chive cream, and you could use purple chive flowers, if available, to garnish. Chives are great for people who don't have room for a garden – plant them in small terracotta pots and keep them on the terrace, or even on a window sill. Cut off the leaves close to the roots – the more you cut, the stronger they grow. The dish will look better if you snip up the leaves with scissors rather than using a knife.

Heat the olive oil in a frying pan, add the shallots and garlic and fry gently until softened. Stir in the sweet potatoes, carrots and thyme. Cover the pan and cook the vegetables for 4 minutes. Stir in the chicken stock and apple juice, bring to a gentle boil and simmer for 20–30 minutes until just soft and tender.

Transfer to a blender or food processor, and purée until smooth. Return the soup to a clean saucepan, taste and adjust the seasoning, then reheat gently. To make the chive cream, mix the chives and flat leaf parsley into the mascarpone and season to taste. Pour the soup into heated soup bowls, place a spoonful of chive cream on each one, then add the chive flowers, if using. Serve with herbed bread rolls or bread sticks.

1 tablespoon olive oil

2 shallots, finely chopped

1 garlic, crushed

500 g/1 lb sweet potatoes, cubed

125 g/4 oz carrots

2 tablespoons chopped fresh lemon thyme leaves

500 ml/1 pint chicken stock

150 ml/¼ pint apple juice

chive flowers, to serve (optional)

chive mascarpone cream

2 tablespoon snipped fresh chives

1 tablespoon chopped fresh flat leaf parsley

5 tablespoons mascarpone

salt and freshly ground black pepper

Serves 4

Couscous salad
with coriander and prawns

Thai fish sauce is available in Asian markets,
gourmet shops or larger supermarkets.

Deseed the cucumber. Diagonally slice the beans,
cucumber and spring onions. Place in a bowl,
sprinkle with the vinegar and leave for 10 minutes.
Reserve the cucumber. Bruise the lemongrass with
the flat of a knife, and place in a bowl with the
couscous and fish sauce. Pour over 300 ml/½ pint
boiling water and soak for 10 minutes. Chop the
herbs and mix with the remaining vegetables and
couscous, pack the mixture into small glasses.
Serve with accompaniments such as rocket leaves,
the reserved cucumber and brown shrimps, if using.

250 g/8 oz green beans

1 bunch of spring onions

1 cucumber, peeled

2 tablespoons vinegar

1 stalk of lemongrass

175 g/6 oz couscous

1 tablespoon fish sauce

1 bunch of coriander

1 bunch of mint

rocket leaves

125 g/4 oz brown
shrimps (optional)

Serves 4

Fresh crab salad
with lemon chervil vinaigrette

Chervil is a member of the parsley family,
with a delicately pretty, feathery leaf. Use
cider vinegar or rice vinegar in this recipe.

Mix the chervil, olive oil, vinegar and honey in a
bowl. Stir in the crab meat, tomatoes and cucumber.
Pack into small cups, place on the plates and serve
with accompaniments such as toasted baguette and
mixed salad leaves.

2 tablespoons chopped
fresh chervil leaves

6 tablespoons olive oil

1 tablespoon vinegar

2 teaspoons honey

250 g/8 oz crab meat

125 g/4 oz cherry
tomatoes, chopped

1 cucumber, chopped

Serves 4

Cucumber mousse
with dill and mixed herb salad

Dill has a mild aniseed taste that marries
well with other cool ingredients like
cucumbers and crème fraîche. This recipe
from *Marie Claire* magazine is light and airy –
ideal as a starter, or as an accompaniment
for smoked fish, eel, halibut or salmon. You
don't have to buy special mousse moulds –
just set them in these chunky French bistro-
style cups or tumblers.

Chop the cucumbers roughly into 5 cm/2 inch
pieces. Place in a pan, just cover with water, simmer
for 3 minutes until soft, then drain. Place in a
blender or food processor, purée for about 1 minute
until just smooth, then transfer to a bowl.
Stir in the crème fraîche, dill, watercress, spring
onions and lemon zest, then add salt, freshly ground
black pepper and the lemon juice.
Dissolve the gelatine in a little water, according to
the packet instructions, and fold into the mousse.
Spoon the mixture into 6 moulds or tumblers.
Chill for about 2 hours. Serve with a light herb salad
dressed with vinaigrette.

3 large cucumbers,
peeled, halved
and deseeded

300 ml/½ pint
crème fraîche

1½ tablespoons
chopped fresh dill

50 g/2 oz watercress,
finely chopped

4 spring onions,
finely chopped

grated zest and
juice of ½ lemon

5 sheets of gelatine

sea salt and freshly
ground black pepper

herb salad with
vinaigrette, to serve

Serves 4

roasted tomatoes have a **heavenly and intense** flavour

that marries well with fresh **basil and oregano**

Basil custard filo tarts
with oregano and roasted tomatoes

Roasting plum tomatoes gives the most heavenly and intense flavour. Oregano is a wild marjoram used widely in Greek and Italian cooking, especially with tomatoes. Like most herbs, it's better used fresh, but if you find the big bunches of dried oregano sold in Greek delicatessens, buy some, if only to make your kitchen smell marvellous.

Place the tomatoes on a baking sheet, dab with olive oil, sprinkle with oregano, sea salt and black pepper. Roast in a preheated oven at 200°C (400°F) Gas Mark 6 for about 15–20 minutes.
To make the filo tart shells, melt the butter and stir in the oregano. Using a pair of scissors, cut the pastry into sixteen 15 cm/6 inch squares.
Brush four 10 cm/4 inch tart tins with the oregano-flavoured butter, then layer 4 sheets of pastry into each tin, brushing each layer with herb butter. Cover with foil and bake blind at 200°C (400°F) Gas Mark 6 for 10–15 minutes until just golden. Remove from the oven and reduce the temperature to 150°C (300°F) Gas Mark 3. Beat the custard ingredients together, then spoon into the tart cases. Return to the oven and cook for 20–30 minutes until just set. Place the warmed roasted tomatoes on top and bake for a further 10 minutes.
Serve warm with a salad of herbs and mustard greens, and a herb vinaigrette.

500 g/1 lb plum tomatoes, halved

1 tablespoon olive oil

2 tablespoons chopped fresh oregano leaves

sea salt and freshly ground black pepper

herby filo pastry

50 g/2 oz butter

1 tablespoon snipped fresh oregano leaves

8 sheets filo pastry

basil custard

1 egg

150 ml/¼ pint double cream

3 tablespoons chopped fresh basil leaves

to serve

salad of mustard greens and assorted herbs

herb vinaigrette

Serves 4

Summer vegetables
with a caper and parsley sauce

Usually teamed with carpaccio (thinly sliced
Italian raw beef) this sauce is also good with
vegetarian dishes. Don't think parsley is
ordinary because it's familiar – it's a great
basic flavour, with a fresh, clean taste.

2 heads of baby fennel

2 courgettes

4 plum tomatoes

4 large spring onions

**caper and
parsley sauce**

4 tablespoons white
wine vinegar

6 gherkins

4 tablespoons chopped
fresh flat leaf parsley

2 garlic cloves

2 anchovy fillets

3 tablespoons capers

1 onion, chopped

175 ml/6 fl oz olive oil

Serves 4

Slice all the vegetables in half lengthways and
arrange on a serving platter.
Place all the sauce ingredients, except the olive oil,
in a blender or food processor, and purée.
With the machine still running, add the oil drop by
drop to make a thick green sauce.
Chill until ready to serve.
Alternatively, roast a selection of vegetables in a
preheated oven at 200°C (400°F) Gas Mark 6 for
about 20 minutes, or until crispy at the edges, then
serve warm with the caper and parsley sauce.

Herbed risotto cakes
with spinach and sage leaf crisps

Risotto is a popular dish – and substantial enough for a main course for lunch. But it also makes an interesting little starter if you serve it in smaller portions as in these little timbales. Deep-fried herb leaves make a wonderful garnish idea. You could also use crisps made from vegetables such as sweet potatoes – a little fiddly to make, but worth the trouble for a special occasion.

To make the risotto, melt the butter and olive oil in a frying pan, add the shallots and gently sauté until soft and tender. Stir in the rice and garlic, cook gently for a few minutes, then stir in the hot stock, one ladle at a time, waiting until each ladleful has been absorbed, before adding the next. Stir in the herbs, then press the rice into 4 moulds or cups, and keep them warm while you prepare the spinach and sage leaf crisps.
To make the crisps, heat the corn oil in a deep-fryer, or in a pan, to 180°C/350°F, or until a cube of bread browns in 30 seconds. Add the spinach leaves, and fry for a few minutes until crisp and tender, then remove and drain on kitchen paper. Repeat with the sage leaves.
Invert the risotto cakes on to individual starter plates, then serve with the sage and spinach crisps.

25 g/1 oz butter

1 tablespoon olive oil

2 shallots, finely chopped

250 g/8 oz risotto rice

1 garlic clove, crushed

350 ml/12 fl oz hot chicken stock

2 tablespoons chopped fresh lemon thyme leaves

1 tablespoon chopped fresh sage leaves

sea salt

spinach and sage leaf crisps

corn oil, for frying

50 g/2 oz spinach leaves

handful of sage leaves

Serves 4

deep-fried **crispy herb leaves** make an unusual garnish

Fish

Breaded mussels
with chives and sage

Sage has a strong, rather smoky taste, which marries well with the assertive flavours of mussels. This recipe is based on an Italian original, in which Italian sausage is mixed with sage then used to stuff the mussels. The shells are then trussed up with chive leaves and baked. You could also make a simpler dish just by mixing the breadcrumbs with a little pesto and lemon juice.

Blanch the chives in boiling water for 1 minute. Drain and run under cold water. This will make them pliable enough to tie up the parcels.

Place the mussels in a dry frying pan just large enough to hold them, then add the white wine. Cover the pan and cook over high heat for 2–3 minutes until the shells are just open.

Heat half the oil in another frying pan, and when hot, add the garlic and sauté gently. Crumble the sausage and add to the pan, then add the breadcrumbs. Season with freshly ground black pepper.

Place a small amount of the breadcrumb mixture inside each mussel and top with a sage leaf. Close the shells and tie each one with a blanched chive. Place the remaining olive oil in a roasting tin, add the mussels and cook in a preheated oven at 190°C (375°F) Gas Mark 5 for 12–15 minutes. Serve with lemon wedges and crusty country bread.

1 bunch of fresh chives

750 g/1½ lb mussels, cleaned

2 tablespoons white wine

2 tablespoons extra-virgin olive oil

2 garlic cloves, crushed

50 g/2 oz fresh Italian pork sausage, skins removed

2 oz/50 g dried breadcrumbs

32 fresh sage leaves

salt and freshly ground black pepper

to serve

lemon wedges

country bread

Serves 4

Salmon with fennel
on mint tabbouleh salad

A recipe that's been given the Pacific Rim treatment, with a mixture of flavours and culinary influences. Lebanese tabbouleh salad is usually made with bulgar wheat – but it's also wonderful made with couscous, that staple of North African cooking.
The pretty fronds of fennel are perfect with salmon. Fennel is easy to grow in the garden – and there is a beautiful bronze variety that tastes as wonderful as it looks. If you can't find the true fennel herb, you could also use the feathery fronds of fennel bulbs – or dill.

Place the couscous in a bowl. Pour over 300 ml/ ½ pint boiling water. Set aside for 10 minutes. Place the salmon fillets and asparagus in a roasting tin. Brush both with olive oil, season with salt and scatter with parsley. Roast in a preheated oven at 200°C (400°F) Gas Mark 6 for 5–7 minutes. Finely slice the spring onions and roughly tear the mint into pieces. Fluff up the couscous with a fork, then stir in the spring onions and mint. Place a spoonful of couscous tabbouleh on each plate, arrange the asparagus and pickled ginger on top, then add the roasted salmon. Mix the fennel dressing ingredients together, sprinkle over the salmon and tabbouleh, then serve. Tie up the asparagus with chive flowers, if using, and sprinkle with sprigs of fennel.

175 g/6 oz couscous

4 slices salmon fillet,
about 5 cm/2 inches wide

250 g/8 oz asparagus
spears, trimmed

2 tablespoons olive oil

2 tablespoons chopped
fresh flat leaf parsley

1 bunch of
spring onions

1 bunch of fresh mint

2 tablespoons
pickled pink ginger
(from Asian food stores)

salt

fennel dressing

4 tablespoons chopped
fresh fennel leaves

1 tablespoon honey

4 tablespoons olive oil

salt and freshly
ground black pepper

to serve

sprigs of fennel

chive flowers (optional)

Serves 4

Pan-fried monkfish
with chermoula marinade

Chermoula is a spicy coriander and parsley marinade from Morocco – great with monkfish, which is firm enough to hold its shape, while still absorbing all the spicy flavours. Stir-fried vegetables or steamed coconut rice would make an interesting multi-cultural accompaniment for this dish.

500 g/1 lb monkfish tail, skinned and boned

2 tablespoon olive oil

chermoula

1 bunch of coriander

1 bunch of parsley

2 garlic cloves, crushed

1 teaspoon ground cumin

1 teaspoon ground paprika

juice of 2 lemons

grated zest of 1 lemon

2 tablespoons olive oil

Serves 4

To make the chermoula, chop all the herb leaves together, using a sharp knife. Place in a bowl, mix in the garlic, cumin, paprika, lemon juice and grated zest, and stir in the olive oil.
Cut the monkfish into slices and place in a shallow dish. Spoon over the chermoula and place in the refrigerator to marinate for at least 30 minutes, or up to 4 hours.
Heat the olive oil in a frying pan, remove the fish from the marinade and gently fry it for about 4 minutes on each side.
Meanwhile, pour the marinade into a pan and heat gently. To serve, place the fish on heated plates and drizzle over the marinade.

Thai sea bass with
ginger and lemongrass glaze

Sea bass is ideal for this dish, but you could also use halibut or cod. Lemongrass, one of the major flavouring ingredients of Thai and Vietnamese cooking, is a relatively new addition to our herb repertoire. It is widely available, but if you can't find it on the same day as you buy the fish, you could double the quantity of lemon juice instead, though the flavour would not be quite the same.

Mix the glaze ingredients together, place the fish in a shallow dish, pour over the marinade and chill for at least 30 minutes or up to 2 hours.
Remove the fish from the marinade and place on a preheated cast-iron stove-top grill, brush with the marinade and cook for about 3 minutes in total.
Heat the oil in a wok or frying pan, add the sliced spring onions, chilli, sugar snap peas and mangetout, then quickly stir-fry.
Meanwhile, gently heat the remaining glaze in a saucepan. To serve, place the fish on heated plates, add the vegetables, drizzle with the glaze and garnish with sprigs of coriander.

500 g/1 lb sea bass, halibut steaks or cod

1 tablespoon sunflower oil

1 bunch of spring onions, sliced

1 red chilli, deseeded and finely sliced

175 g/6 oz sugar snap peas

175 g/6 oz mangetout

sprigs of coriander, to serve

lemongrass glaze

1 tablespoon light brown sugar

1 tablespoon light soy sauce

1 tablespoon lemon juice

2 tablespoons sherry

2 stalks of fresh lemongrass, bruised

2.5 cm/1 inch piece of fresh ginger, peeled and finely diced

1 garlic clove, crushed

Serves 4

Thai-style fish and chips
with coriander dipping sauce

Classic fish and chips are given a modern update with a Thai twist via the coriander – a favourite herb in South-east Asian cooking. Use cod, sole or plaice for this dish, and serve with sweet potato chips. Chips are always better when twice cooked – cook first until golden, drain and deep-fry again until brown and crisp. They're even better made with sweet potato than with ordinary potato.

To make the chips, peel the sweet potatoes and cut into thin slices. Rinse under cold running water and pat dry. Heat the oil in a deep frying pan to about 180°C/350°F, or until a cube of bread browns in 30 seconds. Add the sweet potato and fry until golden. Set aside to keep warm.
Cut the fish into evenly sized strips. To make the batter, whisk the egg white with the salt, then fold in the sesame seeds. Dip the fish first into cornflour, then into the sesame and egg white batter.
Heat the oil in a wok or frying pan to about 180°C/350°F. Add the pieces of fish and gently shallow-fry for about 7–10 minutes until just golden. Meanwhile, reheat the oil in the deep-fryer, add the chips and fry for a second time until brown and crispy. Drain and sprinkle with sea salt. Mix together the dipping sauce ingredients, and serve with the fish and chips.

500 g/1 lb fish fillets

oil, for shallow-frying

sesame batter

1 large egg white

a pinch of salt

1 tablespoon cornflour

2 tablespoons white
sesame seeds

chips

500 g/1 lb sweet
potatoes

groundnut oil, or corn
oil, for deep-frying

sea salt

dipping sauce

3 tablespoons pickled
ginger juice (optional)

1 teaspoon sugar

1 tablespoon
rice vinegar

2–3 tablespoons
chopped coriander

1 red chilli, deseeded
and chopped

2 tablespoons soy sauce

Serves 4

Meat and poultry

Duck breast salad
with coriander and lemongrass

Lemongrass with coriander is a wonderful marriage of flavours, giving a fresh clean taste. Mix them with other Thai-influenced ingredients to give a truly wonderful dish.

Mix the marinade ingredients together, add the duck breasts, and leave to marinate in the refrigerator for up to 24 hours.

Remove the breasts from the marinade, place in a roasting tin, brush with honey and sprinkle with the sesame seeds. Cook in a preheated oven at 200°C (400°F) Gas Mark 6 for 20 minutes. Remove from the oven, set them aside to rest for 5 minutes, then slice.

Soak the noodles in boiling water for 3 minutes, or according to the packet instructions, then drain. Heat the marinade in a small pan, then pour over the cooked noodles. Mix the spring onions and bean sprouts into the noodles

To serve, place the watercress on heated plates, add a pile of noodles and a few slices of the duck breasts, and scatter with fresh basil leaves, if using.

2–4 duck breasts

1 teaspoon honey

1 tablespoon sesame seeds

2 sheets egg noodles

1 bunch of spring onions, sliced diagonally

175 g/6 oz bean sprouts

125 g/4 oz watercress

fresh basil leaves, or Asian basil (optional), to serve

lemongrass marinade

1 tablespoon honey

1 tablespoon Thai fish sauce

2 tablespoon sherry

1 garlic clove, crushed

2 stalks lemongrass, crushed

1 tablespoon fresh coriander, roughly chopped

Serves 4

Tarragon chicken
with herby crème fraîche sauce

Chicken and tarragon are one of the classic combinations, especially in French cooking. Tarragon has a strong, peppery taste, that is also wonderful in pizzas. The Italians rather romantically call it *dragoncello*.

Place the chicken in a casserole dish with the tarragon, parsley, water and seasoning, bring to a gentle simmer and poach for about 20 minutes, or until tender. Cool slightly in the poaching liquid. Remove the chicken from the dish and reserve the poaching liquid to use as stock. Using a knife, take the meat away from the bones, keeping the pieces large and chunky. Heat the olive oil in the casserole dish, and lightly sauté the shallots until softened and transparent. Stir in the flour and cook for 1 minute, to allow the starch grains to burst. Remove from the heat, gradually stir in the reserved stock, little by little, to prevent lumps forming. Return to the heat, bring to the boil and simmer for 1 minute. Stir in the crème fraîche, then add the chicken and chopped herbs. To make the sautéed potatoes, heat the butter and oil in a frying pan and cook the potatoes until golden. Serve with with the chicken and scatter with sprigs of parsley and tarragon.

4 chicken pieces

4 sprigs of tarragon, plus extra to serve

2 sprigs of curly parsley, plus extra to serve

250 ml/8 fl oz water

1 tablespoon olive oil

2 shallots, sliced

1 tablespoon plain flour

250 ml/8 fl oz low-fat crème fraîche

1 teaspoon chopped fresh tarragon

1 tablespoon chopped fresh parsley

salt and freshly ground black pepper

sautéed potatoes

25 g/1 oz butter

1 tablespoon olive oil

500 g/1 lb potatoes, thinly sliced

Serves 4

Chicken breasts
with sorrel, chives and mascarpone

Chicken – low-fat and versatile – is still the most popular meat in the world. You could also replace it with turkey in this recipe – both chicken and turkey are perfect with the light, gentle flavours of herbs. Sorrel is easy to grow in the garden, or even in a window box, and is also available through good greengrocers and larger supermarkets. If unavailable, use baby spinach instead.

4 free-range chicken breasts, skin and bone removed, or turkey escalopes

250 g/8 oz sorrel

3 tablespoon fresh chives, chopped

125 g/4 oz mascarpone

olive oil, for roasting

sea salt and freshly ground black pepper

cooked fresh pasta, to serve

Serves 4

Place the chicken breasts, cut sides up, between two sheets of greaseproof paper on a board. Using a wooden rolling pin, hit hard to flatten the breasts to a thinner and more even texture.
Place the sorrel leaves on top of the breasts. Mix the chives into the mascarpone, and season with salt and pepper. Add 1 tablespoon to each breast, on top of the sorrel, and spread out. Roll up into parcels and secure with cocktail sticks
Place in a roasting tin, drizzle with a little olive oil, sprinkle with sea salt and black pepper and cook in a preheated oven at 200°C (400°F) Gas Mark 6 for about 20–30 minutes.
Serve with fresh pasta made with wild garlic, or plain pasta tossed in parsley pesto.

Pork and lime brochettes
with lemongrass marinade

The wonderful, heady flavours of Thai cuisine,
with wafts of lemongrass, kaffir lime leaves,
and coconut, marry well with chicken or
pork. Kaffir lime leaves are sold in Asian
markets – buy extra and freeze the leftovers
so you always have some on hand.

1 aubergine,
quartered and sliced

750 g/1½ lb pork fillet

2 limes, cut into
wedges

2 kaffir lime leaves
(optional)

**lemongrass
marinade**

2 stalks of lemongrass,
halved and bruised

2 tablespoons mirin
(Japanese rice wine),
or dry sherry

4 tablespoons
coconut milk

2 sprigs of basil

1 garlic clove, crushed

Serves 4

To prepare the marinade, first cut the lemongrass in
half lengthways and bruise by tapping firmly with a
rolling pin or the flat of a heavy knife.
Mix the marinade ingredients together, add the
aubergine and the pork, then chill for 2–12 hours,
depending on the time available.
When ready to cook, remove the aubergine and meat
from the marinade. Thread on to soaked wooden
skewers, alternating with wedges of lime and pieces
of kaffir lime leaves, if using.
Place the brochettes on a hot stove-top grill-pan (or
barbecue) and cook for about 7 minutes, until the
meat is thoroughly cooked.
Steamed coconut rice and a little sweet and sour
dipping sauce would be suitable accompaniments.

Vietnamese pork
stir-fried with pak choy and mint

Pork with in a Pan-Pacific sauce – using flavours of tamarind mixed with spices and mint. Use hot Vietnamese mint, if you can find it, but ordinary mint – especially spearmint – is an acceptable substitute.

Mix the marinade ingredients together, add the pork and leave to marinate for about 2 hours.
Heat half the oil in a pan or wok, remove the pork from the marinade and fry gently. When sealed and brown, stir in the cucumber, stir-fry for a few minutes, then add the marinade, bring to the boil and simmer for 5–10 minutes until thickened.
Cook the egg noodles according to the packet instructions.
Pull the pak choy apart, heat the remaining sunflower oil in a wok or frying pan and stir-fry the pak choy until wilted.
Drain the noodles and serve with the pak choy and pork, scattered with coriander.

500 g/1 lb pork fillet, sliced

2 tablespoons sunflower oil

1 cucumber, peeled, deseeded and sliced diagonally

1 packet dried egg noodles

4 small pak choy

coriander, to serve

tamarind marinade

6 tablespoons tamarind paste

1 garlic clove, chopped

1 teaspoon chilli powder

¼ teaspoon ground ginger

1 bunch of spring onions

1 green chilli, sliced

4 plum tomatoes, finely chopped

2 tablespoons roughly torn leaves of fresh mint

150 ml/¼ pint rice vinegar

Serves 4

Pork and fennel daube
with potato and bay leaf gratin

Fennel has a gentle anise flavour, and the
seeds often form the basis of a curry spice
mix. This recipe uses all three types of
fennel – the herb, the bulb and the seeds.
Herb fennel, especially the pretty bronze
variety, is easily grown in the garden, or you
could substitute the feathery fronds from the
top of the bulb fennel, as shown below.

To prepare the gratin, place the sliced potatoes and
onion in a gratin dish, season with salt and pepper,
add the bay leaves and milk, and brush the top with
melted butter. Set aside until ready to cook the pork.
Heat the oil in a deep casserole dish, add the meat
and brown on all sides. Stir in the fennel seeds,
bacon pieces and onions. Stir in the flour, cook for
1 minute, then stir in the stock and red wine,
tomatoes, fennel pieces and fresh bay leaves.
Place the potato gratin and the pork daube in a
preheated oven and cook at 180°C (350°F) Gas
Mark 6 for 40 minutes.
The pork can also be simmered, covered, on top
of the stove for 50 minutes.
Serve the daube and gratin together.

1 tablespoon olive oil

750 g/1½ lb pork, cut in
2.5 cm/1 inch cubes

2 teaspoons
fennel seeds

4 slices of
streaky bacon

3 onions, sliced

1 tablespoon cornflour

300 ml/½ pint
chicken stock

150 ml/¼ pint red wine

4 plum tomatoes, halved

2 fennel bulbs, sliced

2 fresh bay leaves

sprigs of fennel, to serve

**bay leaf and
potato gratin**

500 g/1 lb potatoes,
thinly sliced

1 onion, thinly sliced

2 bay leaves

150 ml/¼ pint milk

melted butter,
for brushing

Serves 4

Lamb with thyme
and fresh mint vinaigrette

The woody scent of rosemary and thyme
is reminiscent of the beautiful food and
landscapes of the South of France. Lamb is
traditionally combined with these herbs and
also served with a mint vinaigrette.
Steamed vegetables tossed with herbs and
butter are a delicious accompaniment.

Place the lamb in a roasting tin. Using a sharp knife,
cut slits into the meat and insert slices of garlic.
Brush with oil, sprinkle with thyme and cook in a
preheated oven at 190°C (375°F) Gas Mark 5 for
1 hour. To make the vinaigrette, mix the mint with the
salt, pepper, vinegar and olive oil, and set aside.
Clean the carrots, leaving a little of the green tops
intact. To clean the leeks, remove the root and trim
the ragged green leaves. Slit the green part
lengthways and rinse well to remove all the sand.
Scrub the potatoes and boil in salted water for
about 20 minutes. Steam the carrots and leeks in a
steamer over the pan of potatoes, for about
10 minutes, or until just tender.
Reserve 150 ml/¼ pint of the vegetable water.
Drain the vegetables and toss in chives and butter.
To make the gravy, pour off the fat from the roasting
tin, stir in the flour, then add the red wine and the
reserved vegetable water. Boil for a few minutes,
stirring, until thickened. Carve the lamb and serve
with the vinaigrette, vegetables and a little gravy.

½ leg of lamb

1 garlic clove, sliced

olive oil, for brushing

2 tablespoons chopped
fresh thyme leaves

mint vinaigrette

1 large bunch of fresh
mint leaves, chopped

a pinch of sugar

2 tablespoons
red wine vinegar

2 tablespoons olive oil

sea salt and pepper

chive vegetables

250 g/8 oz carrots

500 g/1 lb young leeks

500 g/1 lb new potatoes

2 tablespoons snipped
fresh chives

25 g/1 oz butter

gravy

1 tablespoon plain flour

150 ml/¼ pint red wine

Serves 4

Beef in red wine
with parsley thyme dumplings

This traditional meat dish is cooked with a *bouquet garni,* the French term for a bundle of herbs. In this case, it consists of a bay leaf, thyme and parsley, and gives extra punch to the stew. Parsley and thyme pack the dumplings full of flavour – make them with vegetarian suet for a light finish.

Dip the meat in the seasoned flour, heat the oil in a casserole dish, add the pieces of meat and fry until sealed and browned. Stir in the vegetables, red wine, stock and bouquet garni. Bring to the boil, cover with a lid, place in a preheated oven and cook at 160°C (325°F) Gas Mark 3 for 1 hour. Stir in the seasoning. To make the dumplings, rub the suet into the flour until it resembles fine breadcrumbs. Mix in the herbs, stir in 2–4 tablespoons water and shape the mixture into small golf ball sized dumplings. Place around the top of the casserole and cook, uncovered, for 20–30 minutes more until the dumplings are risen and golden. Serve immediately with vegetables such as buttered cabbage and jacket potatoes with herb butter.

500 g/1 lb chuck steak, cubed

2 tablespoons seasoned flour

2 tablespoons olive oil

250 g/8 oz baby onions

250 g/8 oz baby carrots

150 ml/¼ pint red wine

250 ml/8 fl oz vegetable stock

1 bouquet garni

salt and freshly ground black pepper

herb dumplings

50 g/2 oz vegetarian suet

125 g/4 oz plain flour

2 tablespoons chopped, fresh, flat leaf parsley

2 teaspoons chopped fresh thyme leaves

Serves 4

a traditional dish made with **bouquet garni,**

served with **herb dumplings** to mop up the sauce

Vegetarian dishes

Herbed vegetables
with parsley pesto in a crusty loaf

This delicious crusty loaf filled with grilled
vegetables and pesto is spectacular but easy
to make for lunch or a picnic. Try making
pesto with parsley for a refreshing change.

To make the parsley pesto, place all the ingredients
in a blender and purée to form a smooth paste.
Brush the aubergines, courgettes and tomatoes with
some of the olive oil and grill for about 5–7 minutes
until dark brown.
Cut the top off the loaf and hollow out the middle,
leaving a 2.5 cm/1 inch crust.
Rub the inside surfaces with the cut sides of the
garlic and drizzle with olive oil.
Spread the pesto over the base, add the rocket and
torn basil leaves, then place the vegetables inside
the loaf in layers, seasoning each layer.
Top with a spoonful of pesto and replace
the bread lid. Serve in chunky slices.

175 g/6 oz aubergines,
sliced

175 g/6 oz courgettes,
sliced

4 plum tomatoes, halved

4–6 tablespoons
olive oil

1 loaf of crusty bread

1 large garlic clove,
cut in half

50 g/2 oz rocket

1 bunch of basil

salt and freshly
ground black pepper

parsley pesto

25 g/1 oz parsley

25 g/1 oz pine nuts

25 g/1 oz Parmesan
cheese

125 ml/4 fl oz olive oil

Serves 4

Mini pizzas
with rocket, oregano and olives

You can buy ready-made pizza bases, but it
is always worth making your own to make
sure they're light and crisp. You can also
replace some of the flour with polenta grain
or rye flour, and add some of the firmer
herbs, such as rosemary, thyme or marjoram.
When it comes to pizza toppings, the simpler
the ingredients the better.

To make the pizza dough, mash the yeast with a
pinch of sugar and the warm water until creamy, then
leave to rise for 20 minutes. Place the flour and salt
in a large bowl, stir in the milk, olive oil and creamed
yeast, and mix together to form a sticky dough.
Knead the mixture to form a smooth dough (about
10 minutes), adding extra flour if necessary.
Brush the surface of the dough with oil to prevent a
crust forming, cover the bowl with a tea towel, and
leave in a warm place to rise for about 2 hours.
Knead again to knock all the air out of the dough,
leave to rise for another 40 minutes, then divide
into 4, roll into rounds, and set aside while you
prepare the topping.
To make the topping, scatter the rocket, chopped
herbs and olives over the pizzas, drizzle with olive oil
and sprinkle with sea salt and black pepper.
Bake in a preheated oven at 220°C (425°F) Gas
Mark 7 for 10–15 minutes, or until golden. Serve with
a salad of vine-ripened tomatoes and basil.

home-ma

yo

...zas are a **revelation** – make them with

...oice of toppings – the **simpler the better**

pizza dough

15 g/½ oz fresh yeast

a pinch of sugar

75 ml/3 fl oz
warm water

350 g/12 oz organic
plain flour

½ teaspoon salt

250 ml/9 fl oz
warm milk

2 tablespoon olive oil,
plus extra for brushing

rocket, oregano
and olive topping

50 g/2 oz rocket

1 tablespoon chopped
fresh oregano leaves

1 tablespoon chopped
fresh thyme leaves

50 g/2 oz black olives,
coated in herbs, pitted

olive oil

sea salt and freshly
ground black pepper

Serves 4

Herbed cheese calzone
with asparagus or broccoli

A calzone is a closed pizza with the filling inside, made with the same dough as on page 50–51, though you can also use pastry.

Divide the dough into 4 and roll out into rounds. Mix the remaining ingredients together, divide into 4 and place on one half of each circle. Brush the edges of the dough with water, fold over and press together. Fold over again, to make a firm seal. Cook in a preheated oven at 220°C (425°F) Gas Mark 7 for 15–18 minutes until the edges are just brown, golden and crisp. Serve with a herb and leaf salad.

1 quantity pizza dough (see pages 50–51)

175 g/6 oz goats' cheese, crumbled

175 g/6 oz asparagus or purple-sprouting broccoli, blanched

1 garlic clove, crushed

2 tablespoons chopped fresh marjoram

salt and freshly ground black pepper

Serves 4

Tomato basil sauce
served with fresh pasta

Basil is the herb that seems just made for tomatoes – and it's a combination that will taste even better if you leave the tomatoes to marinate in olive oil and balsamic vinegar.

Place the tomatoes in a saucepan, pour over the olive oil and vinegar, add the pine nuts, then season with salt and pepper. Roughly tear the basil leaves into pieces, add to the tomatoes, then warm through. Cook the pasta in boiling salted water until *al dente*, then drain and serve in pasta bowls, with the tomatoes and basil piled on top.

250 g/8 oz cherry tomatoes, halved

4 tablespoons olive oil

1 tablespoon balsamic vinegar

50 g/2 oz pine nuts, toasted

1 bunch of fresh basil

500 g/1 lb fresh pasta

sea salt and freshly ground black pepper

Serves 4

Marjoram frittata
with courgettes and cheese

A frittata is a chunky Italian omelette, ideal for summer lunches, served in wedges, with a leafy green salad. They can be made with various ingredients, from roasted asparagus to marinated artichokes or steamed new potatoes tossed in chive butter. The possibilities are endless!

8 free-range eggs

2 small courgettes

4 tablespoons chopped fresh marjoram leaves

25 g/1 oz pecorino romano or Parmesan cheese, grated

olive oil, for frying

salt and freshly ground black pepper

Serves 4

Break the eggs into a bowl and beat lightly with a fork. Grate the courgettes and add to the bowl with the marjoram and cheese.
Heat the oil in a 20 cm/8 inch frying pan, then add a ladle of the frittata mixture, tilt the pan to spread the mixture over the pan, then turn the heat to low. When the frittata is set on the underside, place it under a preheated grill to brown.
Tip on to a plate and set aside, while you repeat with the remaining mixture.

Rosemary courgettes
in herb pastry crust

This pie filling mixture of summer squashes with rosemary and Parmesan can also be used as a sauce to serve with pasta.

To make the pastry, place the flour in a bowl, and mix in the remaining ingredients with a fork. Knead rapidly to form a dough, form into a ball, cover with a tea towel, then leave the dough to rest for 1 hour. To make the filling, slice and dice the courgettes and thinly slice the tomatoes. Heat the olive oil in a pan and gently sauté the shallots for about 10 minutes. Mix the crushed garlic with the egg, stir in the courgettes and the remaining ingredients, then season with salt and pepper.

Roll out half of the pastry on a well-floured board, trim to an approximate circle and place on a lightly oiled baking sheet. Spread the filling evenly over the surface to within 1.5 cm/¾ inch of the edge. Roll out the other half of the pastry just wider than the first, fold it and cut a tiny V out of the centre to form a vent. Moisten the edges of the bottom round of pastry, then fold and seal the top into place, pressing all the way around with your finger. Turn the sealed edges upward and inward to form a thick roll.

Brush the surfaces with olive oil and bake in a preheated oven at 200°C (400°F) Gas Mark 6 for 35–45 minutes, until the pastry is rich and golden. Serve warm or cold with a tomato and basil salad.

500 g/1 lb courgettes

4 sun-dried tomatoes

2 tablespoons olive oil

2 shallots, finely sliced

2 garlic cloves, crushed

1 egg, beaten

4 sprigs of rosemary

25 g/1 oz Parmesan cheese

150 ml/¼ pint crème fraîche

sea salt and pepper

herb pastry

250 g/8 oz flour

½ teaspoon chopped fresh oregano

¼ teaspoon chopped fresh thyme

¼ teaspoon chopped fresh rosemary leaves

1 egg

4 tablespoons olive oil

4 tablespoons water

salt

Serves 4

Chard-stuffed onions
with sage and Parmesan sauce

Ideal for a midweek supper dish, baked
onions with a leafy filling of herbs and chard
or spinach, plus a hot béchamel sauce.

Place the unpeeled onions in a pan, cover with water
and boil, uncovered, for 10 minutes. Drain and cool.
Trim off the root and peel off the outer skins. Using a
teaspoon, hollow out the centre so you are left with
2 thick layers for the shell. Roughly chop up the
insides of the onions and reserve for later.
Place 1 teaspoon of the butter in a saucepan and
melt over a moderate heat. Add the Swiss chard,
garlic and sage, and cook gently for 3–4 minutes.
Drain and squeeze out any excess moisture. Place in
a bowl and mix in the chopped onion.
To make the béchamel sauce, melt the butter, stir in
the flour and cook for 1 minute, stirring constantly
until lightly browned. Gradually beat in the milk, a
little at a time, then bring to the boil and simmer
until the sauce thickens.
Reserve 1 tablespoon of the Parmesan and toasted
pine nuts, and mix the remainder into the béchamel,
together with the herb mixture.
Spoon the mixture into the onions, and sprinkle with
the reserved pine nuts and Parmesan.
Pour in the stock and cook in a preheated oven at
180°C (350°F) Gas Mark 4 for about 20 minutes.
Serve immediately with a chicory and watercress
salad and jacket potatoes with herb butter.

8 medium onions,
unpeeled

50 g/2 oz unsalted
butter

350 g/12 oz Swiss chard
(silver beet) or spinach,
steamed, squeezed dry
and chopped

1 garlic clove, crushed

6 sage leaves

50 g/2 oz grated fresh
Parmesan cheese

75 g/3 oz pine nuts,
toasted and chopped

2 tablespoons chopped
fresh sage leaves

2 tablespoons chopped
fresh flat leaf parsley

2 tablespoons olive oil

300 ml/½ pint
chicken stock

sea salt and freshly
ground black pepper

béchamel sauce

25 g/1 oz butter

25 g/1 oz plain flour

250 ml/8 fl oz milk

Serves 4

Sweet things

Windfall apple pie
with lemon thyme

Apple pie is the perfect dish if you have your own apple tree – use sweet windfalls as well as freshly picked ones. No apple tree? Never mind – everyone loves good apple puddings, and this is one of the best. The apples pick up a delicious whisper of lemon thyme flavour.

To make the pastry, sieve the flour into a large bowl, stir in the ground almonds, add the cubes of butter and, using a knife, cut the butter into the flour. Using your fingertips, rub the butter into the flour until it resembles fine breadcrumbs. Add 3–4 tablespoons ice-cold water and bind the mixture together to form a smooth dough. Chill, while you prepare the apples. Place the sliced apples in a pie dish, and mix in the thyme, sugar and water.
Roll out the pastry on a floured surface. Cut small strips of pastry and place round the pie edge, dab with a little cold water, then place the pastry lid on top. Trim off the excess pastry.
Cut a small slash in the centre of the pie, then re-roll the trimmings and cut out pastry leaves. Brush the leaves with water and press on to the top of the pie. Brush milk over the top and place the pie on a baking sheet. Cook in a preheated oven at 180°C (350°F) Gas Mark 4 for 20–30 minutes until the pastry is golden and the apples cooked.

500 g/1 lb apples, peeled, cored and sliced

4 sprigs of lemon thyme

3 tablespoons granulated sugar

2 tablespoons water

milk, for brushing

almond pastry

250 g/8 oz plain flour

1 tablespoon ground almonds

125 g/4 oz unsalted butter, softened and cut into cubes

3–4 tablespoons ice-cold water

Serves 4

Citron tart
with rosemary pastry

Sieve the flour and half the icing sugar together. Soften the butter, then rub into the flour, together with the rosemary. Add the egg yolk and enough cold water to bind the mixture. Chill for 30 minutes. Roll out the pastry and use to line a 23 cm/9 inch flan ring. Prick with a fork, line with greaseproof paper and fill with baking beans. Bake at 200°C (400°F) Gas Mark 6 for 10 minutes. Remove the beans and paper and cook for 10 minutes more. To make the filling, whisk the eggs with the sugar until pale, then add the lemon juice, zest and cream. Pour into the pastry case and bake at 140°C (300°F) Gas Mark 2 for 30 minutes until set. Sprinkle with the remaining icing sugar and serve.

250 g/8 oz plain flour

2 tablespoons icing sugar

125 g/4 oz butter

1 teaspoon chopped fresh rosemary leaves

1 egg yolk

citron filling

3 free-range eggs

175 g/6 oz caster sugar

3 lemons

125 ml/4 fl oz double cream

Serves 4

Lavender biscuits

To make lavender sugar, place 8–12 blossoms in a jar of caster sugar and leave for 2 weeks.

Rub the butter into the flour until it resembles fine breadcrumbs. Add the sugar, lavender and vanilla and knead to a smooth dough. Roll out on a floured surface and cut into rounds with a biscuit cutter. Place on a greased baking tray in a preheated oven at 200°C (400°F) Gas Mark 6 for 8–10 minutes until golden. Cool for 2 minutes, then transfer to a wire rack. Decorate with melted chocolate and serve.

125 g/4 oz butter

175 g/6 oz plain flour

75 g/3 oz caster sugar or lavender sugar

1 teaspoon dried lavender, chopped

2 drops vanilla essence

50 g/2 oz plain chocolate, melted

Serves 4

two unusual baking recipes, packed with **herb** flavours

Index

A

apple pie, windfall, with lemon thyme 61
Asian mint 9

B

basil 6, 8, 17, 32, 38, 49, 52
    Asian basil 32
    basil custard filo tarts with oregano and roasted tomatoes 17
bay leaf 6, 42
beef in red wine with parsley thyme dumplings 47
biscuits, lavender 62
breaded mussels with chives and sage 23
brochettes, pork and lime, with lemongrass marinade 38

C

calzone, herbed cheese, with asparagus or broccoli 52
chard-stuffed onions with sage and Parmesan sauce 60
chermoula marinade 26
chervil 6, 8, 12
chicken
    breasts with sorrel, chives and mascarpone 37
    tarragon, with herby crème fraîche sauce 34
chive flowers 11
chives 6, 8, 11, 23, 37, 44
citron tart with rosemary pastry 62
coriander 6, 9, 12, 26, 29, 30, 33, 40
couscous salad with coriander and shrimps 12
crab salad, fresh, with lemon chervil vinaigrette 12
crisps, spinach and sage leaf, herbed risotto cakes with 20
cucumber mousse, dill and, with mixed herb salad 14

D

daube, pork and fennel, with tomato and onions 42
dill 6, 8, 14
    cucumber mousse with dill and mixed herb salad 14

duck breast salad with coriander and lemongrass 33
dumplings, parsley thyme 47

F

fennel 8, 24, 42
filo tarts, basil custard, with oregano and roasted tomatoes 17
fish
    pan-fried monkfish with chermoula marinade 26
    salmon with fennel on mint tabbouleh salad 24
    Thai sea bass with ginger and lemongrass glaze 29
    Thai-style fish and chips with coriander dipping sauce 30
frittata, marjoram, with courgettes and cheese 54

H

herbed cheese calzone with asparagus or broccoli 52
herbed risotto cakes with spinach and sage leaf crisps 20
herbed vegetables with parsley pesto in a crusty loaf 49

K

kaffir lime leaves 6, 38

L

lamb with thyme and fresh mint vinaigrette 44
lavender 6, 8, 62
    biscuits 62
lemongrass 6, 9, 12, 29, 33, 38
lemon thyme 11, 61
lime leaves, kaffir 6, 38

M

marjoram 8, 52, 54
    frittata with courgettes and cheese 54
mascarpone cream, sweet potato soup with chive 11
mini pizzas with rocket, oregano and olives 50
mint 6, 9, 12. 25, 40, 44
monkfish with chermoula marinade, pan-fried 26
mousse, cucumber, with dill and mixed herb salad 14

mussels, breaded, with chives and sage 23

O

onions, chard-stuffed, with sage and Parmesan sauce 60
oregano 6, 8, 17, 51, 57

P

parsley 6, 8, 11, 18, 22, 23, 24, 25, 26, 34, 47, 49, 60
pasta, tomato and basil sauce with fresh 52
pesto 6, 49
pies
    rosemary courgettes in herb pastry 57
    windfall apple, with lemon thyme 61
pizzas
    calzone, herbed cheese, with asparagus or broccoli 52
    mini, with rocket, oregano and olives 50
pork
    and fennel daube with tomato and onions 42
    and lime brochettes with lemongrass marinade 38
    Vietnamese, stir-fried, with pak choy and mint 40

R

risotto cakes, herbed, with spinach and sage leaf crisps 20
rosemary 6, 8, 57, 62
    courgettes in herb pastry crust 57

S

sage 6, 20, 23, 60
salads
    couscous salad, with coriander and shrimp 12
    dill and cucumber mousse with mixed herb salad 14
    duck breast salad with coriander and lemongrass 33
    fresh crab salad, with lemon chervil vinaigrette 12
    mint tabbouleh salad, salmon with fennel on 24
salmon with fennel on mint tabbouleh salad 24
sauces and vinaigrettes
    caper and parsley sauce 18

chermoula marinade 26
chive mascarpone cream 11
coriander dipping sauce 30
fennel dressing 24
fresh mint vinaigrette 44
ginger and lemongrass glaze 29
herby crème fraîche sauce 34
lemon chervil vinaigrette 12
lemongrass marinade 33, 38
parsley pesto 49
sage and Parmesan sauce 60
tomato and basil sauce 52
sea bass, Thai, with ginger and lemongrass glaze 29
seafood
    breaded mussels with chives and sage 22
    fresh crab salad with lemon chervil vinaigrette 12
    couscous salad with coriander and shrimps 12
    soup, sweet potato, with chive mascarpone cream 11
    summer vegetables with a caper and parsley sauce 18
    sweet potato soup with chive mascarpone cream 11

T

tabbouleh 24
tarragon 6, 9, 34
    tarragon chicken with herby crème fraîche sauce 34
tarts
    basil custard filo, with oregano and roasted tomatoes 17
    citron with rosemary pastry 62
    Thai sea bass with ginger and lemongrass glaze 29
    Thai-style fish and chips with coriander dipping sauce 30
thyme 6, 8, 20, 44, 47, 51, 57
    lemon thyme 11,
tomato and basil sauce with fresh pasta 52

V

Vietnamese pork stir-fried with pak choy and mint 40

W

windfall apple pie with lemon thyme 61